## HOW TO HALT A HICCUP

## and Other Handy Hints for Kids

Do you know how to charm a wart? Or
how to greet the Queen? Do you know
how to deal with the class bully or how
to tell if a crocodile is asleep?

The answers to all these problems and
more can be found in this simply
brilliant book!

# HOW TO HALT A HICCUP
## and Other Handy Hints for Kids

**Mary Danby**

**Illustrated by Scoular Anderson**

KNIGHT BOOKS
Hodder and Stoughton

Copyright © Mary Danby, 1990

Illustrations copyright © Hodder and Stoughton Ltd, 1990

First published in Great Britain in 1990 by Knight Books

**British Library C.I.P.**

Danby, Mary, *1941–*
How to halt a hiccup.
1. Activities for children
I. Title   II. Anderson, Scoular
790.1'922

ISBN 0-340-51793-X

Photoset by Rowland Phototypesetting Ltd, Bury St Edmunds, Suffolk. Printed and bound in Great Britain for Hodder and Stoughton Children's Books, a division of Hodder and Stoughton Ltd, Mill Road, Dunton Green, Sevenoaks, Kent, TN13 2YA (Editorial Office: 47 Bedford Square, London WC1B 3DP) by Richard Clay Ltd, Bungay, Suffolk.

# CONTENTS

# Part One
# HOME, SCHOOL AND HOLIDAYS

## AEROPLANES

If your ears become blocked on aeroplanes – usually just before landing – try one of these:

Suck a sweet
Yawn
Hold your nose and blow

Above all, don't let it worry you too much, even if it hurts a bit. Very soon after the plane has landed, your ears will be back to normal.

## AIR BEDS

Don't *ever* lie on an airbed on the sea unless it is very securely tethered to the land.

## APOSTROPHES

Should it be 'its' or 'it's'? Here's a way to remember the rule:
When you write 'it's', the apostrophe shows there's a letter missing (i), so 'it's' means 'it is'.
'Its' comes before something's possession ('its roof', 'its colours', 'its name'). Like 'my' ('my roof'), 'your' ('your colour'), his ('his name'), 'her', 'our' and 'their', 'its' has no apostrophe.

## BALLOONS

Blowing up balloons is easier if you first rub them between your palms and stretch them.

*Rub it on a woollen surface . . .*

To make a balloon cling to a wall or ceiling, rub it first on a woollen surface.

For some fun party invitations, blow up balloons and write the invitations on them in smudge-proof ink. Deflate them, put them in envelopes and post or deliver them. Your guests will have to blow them up to read them.

## BALLPOINT PENS
If your ballpoint pen won't write and it hasn't run out of ink, lightly rub an eraser over a piece of paper, then write on that. It should get the ink flowing more smoothly.

A messy pen point can be cleaned by sticking it into dry earth around a pot plant.

Ballpoint ink stains can be removed from your hands with a small amount of margarine and a damp cloth.

## BANANAS
If you keep bananas in the fridge, their skins will go black but the insides will stay firm for much longer.

You can ripen a green banana faster by putting it next to a ripe banana.

## BATHS
When running a bath, always run some cold water before you turn on the hot tap, and you will be less likely to scald yourself.

Add a little washing-up liquid to your bath and you'll avoid a tidemark.

For a colourful bathtime, run a bubble bath and add a few drops of food-colouring to the water.

## BATTERIES
Weak batteries can often be made to work for a little longer if you sit them on a warm radiator for a few hours.

*Keep cool . . .*

## BEACHES
Keep cool on the beach by digging a shallow pit in the sand and lying in it.

## BELTS
The flapping end of a belt that's lost its 'keeper' can be held in place with Blu-tack.

## BIKES
If you're always leaving your bike out in the rain, give it a wipe over with petroleum jelly to protect it from rust.

Here's how to mark your bicycle so that, if it's stolen, you can prove it's yours, even if it's been resprayed and the serial number's been filed off. Simply write your name and address on a long thin piece of card, then remove the seatpost, drop the card into the bike frame, replace the seatpost and tighten it.

## BIRDS
To prevent your pet bird being troubled by lice, hang a leaf of tobacco in its cage.

If there's a tumble dryer in your house, save the lint from it and put it out for the birds in spring. They love to line their nests with it.

*Don't* put out hard bird food (bacon rind, nuts, seeds etc.) in late spring. If the parent birds take it back to their nests it can choke the babies.

## BISCUITS
To help biscuits stay crisp, keep a couple of lumps of sugar in the biscuit tin. They'll absorb any moisture.

## BOLTS
A rusted bolt can often be loosened by wiping it with a cloth soaked in any kind of fizzy drink.

## BOOKMARKS
An ordinary paperclip makes a very good bookmark – much better for the book than leaving it open face down or turning down a corner.

## BOOKS
Second-hand books, which can often be bought for just a few pence, can make very good presents, if chosen with care.

To mend a torn page in a book, carefully position the edges of the tear together, and smear both sides of the paper with egg white. Let the egg white dry thoroughly before you touch the page again.

## BOOKSHELVES
Make instant bookshelves by resting planks of wood on bricks. Don't build your shelves more than three or four bricks high, though, or they'll be unsteady.

## BREAD
Very fresh bread is easier to slice if it's been kept in the fridge.

To cut a straight slice try keeping your eye on the loaf, rather than the piece you're cutting.

## BREAKABLES
If you collect small china ornaments, it's a good idea to wash them from time to time. Hold a plastic bag over the sink and half fill it with warm water and a little washing-up liquid.
   Place the ornaments one at a time into the bag and shake it gently to loosen any dirt. Let the ornaments drip-dry on a towel placed on the draining board.

You're on holiday and you buy a china or glass souvenir, but you're worried about how to pack it. Try this: wrap it carefully in sheets of very damp paper, covering each part with several layers. Allow time for the paper to dry, and it will stiffen into a firm shell around the souvenir.
   When you get home, remove the paper by soaking it in water.
   Another good way to deal with very small, breakable items is to wrap them up in slices of bread, secured with sticky tape.

## BREAKFAST
Never miss out on breakfast. Your body needs something to get it working in the morning – even just a bowl of cereal.

## BRUISES

Rub a cut leek against a bruise to ease the pain. The juice of the leek will also help to reduce any swelling.

## BUDGIES

If you want to buy a budgie that you can teach to talk, make sure it's less than three months old. You will notice that older birds have a white ring around the eye, or black spots on their throats.

To keep a budgie happy if you have to go out all day, leave the radio on (not too loud). It'll feel less lonely.

Come on, say: 'Who's a pretty boy?'

*Make sure it's less than three months old . . .*

If you need to pick up a budgie (to clip its claws, for instance), turn off the light for a few minutes beforehand to calm it down. You should then be able to catch it quite easily.

## BULLS
If you are charged by a bull, throw something in its path, like your anorak. While it stops to examine this strange object, you can make your escape!

## BURNS
If you burn your fingers, immediately hold them under cold running water, which will quickly lower the temperature and reduce the pain.

## BUTTER
Butter that's too hard for spreading can be softened by putting it in a microwave oven for just a few seconds. But don't forget to check with an adult first about the suitability of its container.

## CAKES
To make a pretty pattern on a chocolate cake, place a paper doily on the top, then sprinkle on some icing-sugar. Remove the doily very carefully and a pretty lace design should be left behind.

Polo mints make fun holders for cake candles.

To ice cup-cakes, simply dip them into the icing and lift them out with a quick twirl.

To make a delicious frosting for cup-cakes, take the cakes from the oven when they're almost done, pop a marshmallow on the top of each cake, then put them back in the oven for a couple of minutes.

Use up left-over icing by spreading it between plain biscuits.

## CAMPING
Always leave an opening somewhere in your tent. If it's too well closed up the vapour given off by your body will make the bedding damp.

If you're camping on a cold night wear a hat in bed. Most of our body heat escapes through our head, so a hat helps to keep it in.

*Wear a hat in bed . . .*

17

Don't touch the sides of the tent when it's raining, or the water will come in. If it leaks, draw a finger down the inside wall of the tent to divert the water.

Cold comes up from the ground, so more bedding is needed underneath than on top. If necessary put a layer of bracken or straw under your bed to insulate it.

To remove a bee from a tent, hold up a flower. When the bee settles on the flower, just carry the flower gently outside.

Keep milk and butter cool by tying them up securely in a plastic bag and suspending it in a stream.

Or keep milk bottles covered with a cloth in a bowl of cold water. The ends of the cloth should touch the water.

Save your potato peelings and dry them out. They make good firelighters.

Use one tent peg to remove another. Hold it upside down and use it to hook the other one out of the ground.

## CARROTS
A slice off the top end of a carrot will sprout green 'ferns' if you stand it in a saucer of water.

## CATS
To teach your cat to come when you call, shake a bowl of biscuits (or make some other noise) every time you give it a treat. Whenever it hears this noise, it'll come running.

If your cat is very naughty and keeps scratching the furniture or jumping up on the kitchen worktops, don't smack it – say 'No!' very firmly and spray or flick a little bit of water at it. The water won't hurt, and the cat will quickly learn.

Cream gives cats indigestion.

To amuse a kitten, crumple a piece of foil and let him bat it around the floor.

To keep cats away from your favourite flowers, spread holly leaves around the base of the plant.

*Keep cats away . . .*

## CAR SICKNESS

Oddly enough, one remedy for this is sucking sweets.

Another is to try wearing sunglasses (the darker the better).

*Use a big paperclip . . .*

## CHEWING-GUM
To remove chewing-gum from your clothes, put the garment in the freezer. Once the gum has hardened, you can pull it off quite easily.

To remove it from your hair or skin, rub in some peanut butter, or harden the gum with ice-cubes before trying to pull it off.

## CHILBLAINS
If you suffer from chilblains, never wear damp gloves or wet socks. Try to keep your hands and feet warm all the time.

## CHRISTMAS
Display your Christmas cards by slipping the backs between books on a bookshelf.

Keep the colourful plastic twisters that sometimes come with wrapped bread and use them to hang ornaments on Christmas trees.

Make Christmas gift tags by cutting up old Christmas cards with pinking shears.

## CLIPS
For a fun paperclip – use a butterfly hairclip.

For a fun hairclip – use a big paperclip.

## CLOTHES
Try to avoid wearing two different patterns together. For instance, patterned shorts usually look best with a plain top. As a general rule, mix plain and plain, or plain and pattern, but never pattern with pattern.

*Never mix pattern with pattern . . .*

Clothes with vertical (up-down) stripes tend to make you look thinner, while horizontal (side-to-side) stripes make you look fatter.

Several layers of thin clothing are warmer than one thick one because they trap air between the layers. (You can also remove them bit by bit if the weather gets warmer.)

## COCA-COLA
Don't throw away Coca-Cola that's gone flat – add it to the wash, to help remove greasy stains from clothes.

## COINS
An old 35mm film container is good for storing or carrying coins. It will hold all coins except 50p pieces.

## COLD FEET
If you suffer from cold feet, try to keep your ankles specially warm. Towelling wristbands make a good extra layer. You might even start a new fashion!

If your feet do get cold, stand on tiptoe to help the blood reach your toes.

Hint for pony-riders: If your feet get very cold, take them out of the stirrups and hang your legs down with your toes pointing at the ground. (Don't do this on the move if you think you might fall off!)

## COMPASS POINTS
If you can never remember, when looking at a map, that West is left and East is right, remind yourself that they spell WE not EW.

## CORKS
To replace a cork in a bottle, when it's a very tight fit, first soak the cork in a little hot water to soften it.

Hang your legs down . . .

## CORNFLAKES
If your cornflakes (or crisps) have gone soggy, spread them out on a baking sheet and pop them in a warm oven (not too hot) for a short time to crisp them up.

## CREAM CRACKERS
Cream crackers tend to crack when you butter them. Try placing them on a slice of bread – it acts as a shock absorber.

## CRISPS
Save the crumbs at the bottom of the bag and add them to salads for a lovely crunchy taste.

*Creep on by . . .*

## CROCODILES

When you come across a crocodile lying on a river bank with its eyes closed and want to find out whether or not it's asleep, look at its legs. If they're pointing backwards along its body, just creep on by. If they're out to the sides, run!

## CURRY

If a curry is too hot and spicy for you, cool it down by adding plain yogurt.

## CUTS

A small cut on your finger will heal quickly if you press a piece of onion skin over it. A few moments of pressure and the inside of the onion skin will stick to your finger. Onions contain a kind of antiseptic, to fight off germs, and when the cut is healed, the onion skin can be gently washed off.


## DAISIES
If rain is on the way, daisies close their petals.

## DATES
Two dates to remember:

> In fourteen hundred and ninety-two,
> Columbus sailed the ocean blue.

*(The discovery of America)*

> In sixteen hundred and sixty-six,
> London was burnt to rotten sticks.

*(The Great Fire of London)*

## DENTISTS
When you're sitting in a dentist's chair, it can be hard to relax your jaw. Try relaxing your hands, and you'll probably find your jaw relaxes too.

## DICE
A dice missing from a game can be replaced with a sugar cube. Use a felt-tip pen to draw the dots, remembering that the opposite faces should always add up to seven.

## DIET
Trying to slim? About 15 minutes before each meal, eat an apple. It will fill you up a bit, so that you're satisfied with a smaller meal.

## DIRT
If you're doing a dirty job without gloves, first scratch a piece of soap with your nails, leaving the pieces of soap

*Rub it well into your skin . . .*

under your nails. Your nails will stay clean and won't become clogged with dirt.

To get rid of dirt and grease when you have no soap, try mud. Rub it well into your skin and rinse it off thoroughly.

## DISPLAYS
An old wooden cutlery box fixed to a wall makes a good display case for small objects.

To make a display wall in your bedroom, hang a big piece of garden netting from picture hooks. Use clothes pegs to pin up pictures, hats, record sleeves – anything you like.

## DOGS

If your dog runs away from you and won't come when you call, try keeping quiet. So long as he can hear your voice, he'll feel quite safe to carry on with whatever he's doing. But if he isn't quite sure where you are he's likely to get anxious and come looking for you.

If your dog's coat smells awful, try rubbing tomato juice into his fur, then rinsing it out thoroughly.

In winter, if it's too cold to give your dog a bath, you can 'dry clean' him by rubbing bicarbonate of soda or baking powder into his coat, then giving him a good brushing.

*You can 'dry clean' your dog . . .*

To clean a dog's muddy paws, rinse them off one at a time in a jam jar of water.

When brushing a long-haired dog, dampen your brush first, to make untangling easier.

Want to produce a beautiful shine on a short-haired dog? First groom it as usual, then stroke it firmly with an old silk scarf.

If a dog is behaving as though it may attack you, avoid looking it in the eye and keep as quiet as you can.

## DRAWING

The easiest way to draw a circle is to draw round something. All kinds of objects are circular – from thimbles to dinner plates, so you should be able to find something that's the size you want.

If you have trouble drawing people, draw a stick person first, then draw on the clothes.

When drawing cartoon faces, don't forget the eyebrows – they are very important to a person's expression. Draw them high or arched for delight or surprise, low and v-shaped for anger or puzzlement.

## DRAWING PINS

Drawing pins are easier to remove if they've been pushed in slightly crooked.

## DRESSING-UP

If you enjoy dressing-up or putting on plays, look in jumble sales for good items for your costume collection. All kinds of amazing hats, jackets and so on can often be picked up very cheaply.

*Draw round something . . .*

## DOLLS' HOUSES
Use wide velvet ribbon for a dolls' house stair carpet.

## DRYING UP
*How to get out of doing the drying up:* Tell your parents it's more hygienic to let the dishes drip dry on the draining-board.

*Male or female . . . ?*

## DUCKLINGS
*How to tell if a duckling is male or female:* At four months old, one of the tail feathers of a drake is folded into a tight curl, while those of a duck are all straight.

## EGG BOXES
Egg boxes make very good seed trays – especially the cardboard ones. Fill them with compost and plant one seed in each section.

## EGGS

To find out if an egg is fresh, place it in a bowl of cold water. If it sinks to the bottom, it's fresh; if it rises in the water, throw it away – it's bad.

A handful of grass in the water in which eggs are boiled will turn their shells green.

Onion skins placed in boiling water will dye eggs all shades from light orange to dark maroon, depending on the amount used.

## EXERCISE BOOKS

A piece of coloured tape on the spine of an exercise book will make it easy to find when it's in the middle of a big pile.

## FACE PAINTS

Home-made face paints can be made by mixing two teaspoonfuls of face cream and a few drops of food colouring. The face paints come off easily with soap and water.

## FAINTING

If you feel faint, the best thing to do is to sit down with your head between your knees. This will restore the blood to your brain. If you can't do this, try pinching your cheeks.

## FEET

Going barefoot is extremely good for your feet, as it exercises and strengthens all the muscles.

To remove sand from your feet, sprinkle them with talcum powder, then rub lightly with a towel. All the sand will vanish.

## FELT-TIP PENS

Felt-tip pens should be stored with the points down, to keep them from drying out.

To make a felt-tip pen last a bit longer, put a few drops of vinegar down the barrel and the colour will start to run again.

To re-charge a felt-tip pen, stand it, point downwards, in a bottle of coloured ink for a few days.

## FIR CONES

To make a fir cone open out, leave it in a warm place. You can give fir cones a sparkle by soaking them in strongly salted water for about half an hour. They will have a frosted appearance when dry.

## FIZZY DRINKS

To fizz up your glass of squash, use soda water instead of tap water.

You can put the fizz back into a flat drink by adding a pinch of bicarbonate of soda (baking powder) and shaking the bottle *very gently* with your thumb over the top. *Do not put a screw cap on the bottle*, in case it explodes. Drink at once.

## FLIES

To keep flies and mosquitoes away, rub your face, arms and legs with fresh mint.

If you're kept awake by a loudly buzzing fly in your bedroom, invite it to leave by opening your bedroom door, switching on a light outside and switching off your bedroom light. The fly will always go towards the light.

*Invite it to leave . . .*

## FLOATING

If you fall in some water and can't swim, the important thing is not to panic and thrash about, as this will send water up your nose and into your mouth. If you stay calm and 'bicycle' with your legs while moving your arms very gently, you'll stay afloat. It's important to keep your arms *under* the water.

## FLOWERS

To arrange a vase of flowers when all they seem to want to do is flop all over the place, tie them in a pretty bunch with string or a rubber band before putting them in the vase.

If flower stems are too short, slip them into plastic drinking straws.

If you are arranging a small number of flowers, an odd number tends to look better than an even number.

To keep a bunch of flowers fresh, wrap the stems first in damp kitchen paper, then in foil.

## FRECKLES
If you have freckles and don't like them (though they are often very attractive) try patting buttermilk on to them. It may help to 'cool them down'.

## GARDENING
Carrot flies hate onions and onion flies hate carrots, so plant carrots next to onions and you won't be bothered by either!

## GERBILS
If you want somewhere to put a gerbil while you clean out its cage, try the bath. It won't be able to climb up the slippery sides.

## GIFT TAGS
Cut out a strip of wrapping paper and fold it in half to make a matching gift tag.

## GLASS
If you have to pick up broken glass, *be very careful*. If the pieces are small, press a thick slice of bread on to them. They will stick into the bread, and the whole thing can be wrapped up safely and placed in a bin.

'Here Comes the Bride . . .'

## GLASSES

To carry a glass or a mug full of liquid without spilling any, try singing 'Here Comes the Bride' and walking slowly along in time with the tune – it helps you to keep steady!

If two glasses are stuck together, fill the top one with cold water and stand the bottom one in hot water. The bottom one will expand slightly, and they'll come apart easily.

## GLOVES

If you are always leaving your gloves behind, get into the habit of saying, whenever you leave somewhere, 'Goodbye,' (then add, under your breath) 'from me and my gloves.' Every time you say goodbye to someone you'll remember your gloves.

To dry wet gloves, pull each one over the bottom of a small empty jar and stand the open ends of the jars on something warm.


## GLUING

Use bulldog clips to clamp objects firmly together while glue is drying.


## GUINEA PIGS

When keeping guinea pigs (or mice), never put two males in the same cage. They're sure to fight.

Sometimes guinea pigs' teeth break off. If you have a toothless guinea pig it will enjoy a meal of unsalted mashed potato.


## HAIR

To untangle long hair painlessly, comb it gently under water.

To make your hair shine, shampoo and rinse it well, then rinse it again with two teaspoons of fresh lemon juice in a bowl of cold water.

If your hair is greasy and there's no time to wash it, you can use cornflour as a dry shampoo. Rub a little cornflour into your hair, then brush it out thoroughly.

*If you have a toothless guinea pig . . .*

## HAIRSPRAY
Hairspray is great for removing glue from your hands. Just spray it on, then rinse off with a wet cloth.

## HAMSTERS
*How to catch an escaped hamster:* Make a hole in the lid of a shoebox that you've lined with crumpled newspaper. Cover the hole with a paper towel and place some food on the towel. When the hamster is hungry, he'll go to the food and drop through the hole into the box.

## HEADACHE
If you have a headache, fill a small plastic bag with ice-cubes and hold it against your forehead (but tell a grown-up, as well).

*Hold it against your forehead . . .*

## HEDGEHOGS
To encourage night-time visits from hedgehogs, put out a little tinned dog food on a saucer. They prefer this to bread and milk (which often gives them diarrhoea).

*Put out a little tinned dog food . . .*

## HICCUPS
*Cures for hiccups:*

Drink a teaspoonful of vinegar.

Drink water from the wrong side of the glass, by tipping your head over the top of the glass.

Hold your breath.

Eat a small piece of ice.

Spreadeagle yourself flat against a door or wall, keeping your head very upright, and ask someone to give you sips of water.

Get someone to give you a sudden shock.

Pat your head with one hand while rubbing your stomach in a circle with the other hand.

Take a mouthful of water, put your fingers in your ears, then swallow.

## HOLLY

To keep holly fresh over Christmas, stick it into large potatoes. A big ball of holly, based on a potato, looks great. You can hang the ball by threading a length of ribbon through the potato.

## HOMEWORK

It's best to do your homework as soon as you get home, then you can relax. It's much harder to work once your mind has switched off.

If you're trying to learn something by heart, do it in short bursts, with breaks in between for walking around, having a snack, etc.

## HOT WEATHER

To cool yourself down in hot weather, run cold water over the insides of your wrists.

## ICE-CUBES

If your soup or drink is too hot, and you're in a hurry, put an ice-cube or two in it.

To make quick jelly, use only half the amount of boiling water stated, and make up the rest with ice-cubes.

The inserts from chocolate boxes can be used to make fun-shaped ice 'cubes'.

To make party ice-cubes, add a tiny drop of food colouring to the water in each section of the tray. Orange juice can be frozen in cubes and used in drinks, too.

## ICE-LOLLY STICKS

Save ice-lolly sticks – they make good glue spreaders or plant labels. Or you can even use them to make your own ice-lollies. (But wash them well first.)

## ICE SKATING
To help yourself skate smoothly and rhythmically, sing a waltz in your head.

## ILLNESS
If you are ill in bed, ask someone to fix up a mirror so that you can see what's going on outside your window.

## INSECTS
Ants will not cross a line drawn in chalk. (You may not need to know that, but it's interesting anyway.)

*Ants will not cross a chalk line . . .*

To remove an insect or a spider, you need a glass and a piece of stiff paper. Put the glass over the insect and feed the paper between the rim of the glass and the surface the insect is standing on, so that the creature is trapped.

Holding the paper firmly against the glass, take the glass outside, uncover it and let the insect or spider climb out. (If you can't stand the sight of spiders, use a plastic beaker.)

## ITCHING
You can sometimes stop an itch by rubbing it with orange or lemon peel.

Rub itchy bites with a wet bar of soap to remove the itch.

## JARS
To open a jar with a tight-fitting lid, wear rubber gloves so your hands don't slip.

## JEANS
You can turn ordinary jeans into ski pants by spraying them with a waterproof fabric protector.

Use a dark blue felt-tip pen to hide the white lines on let-down jeans.

If your jeans are too tight to fasten easily, lie down to zip them up. If that doesn't help, try using the hook on a coat hanger. Thread it through the catch on the zip, then pull on the coat hanger.

## JELLYFISH

To protect yourself from box jellyfish, whose stings are very painful and often fatal, wear tights (as do lifeguards on Bondi beach in Australia).

## JEWELLERY

If a fine neck chain is tightly knotted, place it in a saucer of cooking oil. Use two pins to undo it, then wash it in warm soapy water and dry it.

To keep a fine gold or silver chain from tangling during storage, cut a drinking straw to half the length of the chain, slip the chain through and fasten the catch.

A stuffed animal toy makes a good alternative to a jewellery box. Hang necklaces round its neck and bracelets round its ears. Pin other jewellery on to its body.

## JIGSAWS

When you open a new jigsaw, put a coloured dot on the back of each piece. That way if your jigsaws get mixed up, you'll be able to sort them out into their different colours.

## JUMPING

If you have to jump down from a first-floor window (in a fire, for instance), first hang by your hands from the window-sill, so that your feet are as near the ground as possible.

*Ink can be removed with tomato ketchup . . .*

## KETCHUP

Fountain pen ink on your fingers can be removed with tomato ketchup.

*Remember: shake the ketchup bottle,*
*Or none'll come – and then the lot'll!*

If ketchup refuses to come out of the bottle, push in a drinking straw, to let in some air.

## KETTLES

When making a hot drink, never take the hot kettle to the mug or teapot – *always* take *them* to the kettle.

## KNITTING
Play music while you're knitting and you'll find yourself working to a rhythm, which means your knitting will be more even.

If you have to leave your knitting in mid-row, hold the needles together with a clothes-peg so you don't drop any stitches.

To re-use wool from an old garment, unravel it and wind it tightly round a piece of smooth wood or stiff card. Dip it in luke-warm water and leave it to dry. That way it will lose its kinks.

## LEARNING
Need to learn something by heart? Stick it to the back of the loo door. Every time you visit the toilet, learn one more line.

If you're learning all about a particular subject, try saying out loud all you know about it. Your dog will probably be fascinated!

## LEMON JUICE
This makes good invisible ink. Use it with a clean nib, and hold the paper somewhere warm to see the writing gradually appear.

## LIGHTNING
If you are in a wide open space in a thunderstorm, lie down flat on your stomach. Keep well away from trees.

## LUNCH BOXES
Keep your old plastic lunch boxes. They make very good carrying cases for Lego or cassette tapes, for instance.

## MARKING

Always make sure you mark your belongings with your name, or at least your initials. This will deter thieves, and it also means you can prove the objects are yours.

Use pin pricks to mark your name on a rubber.

Pencils can be marked by cutting a slice off the blunt end and writing your name or initials on the bare wood. Ask an adult for help with cutting the wood.

## MATHS

How's your nine times table? If you're not sure you've got the answers right, just remember this: IF YOU MULTIPLY A NUMBER BY 9, THE FIGURES IN THE ANSWER ALWAYS ADDS UP TO NINE OR A MULTIPLE OF NINE.

*The answer always adds up to nine . . .*

For instance:

$2 \times 9 = \phantom{00}18 \; (1 + 8 = \mathbf{9})$

$15 \times 9 = \phantom{00}135 \; (1 + 3 + 5 = \mathbf{9})$

$437 \times 9 = \phantom{0}3933 \; (3 + 9 + 3 + 3 = \mathbf{18} = 2 \times 9)$

$5261 \times 9 = 47349 \; (4 + 7 + 3 + 4 + 9 = \mathbf{27} = 3 \times 9)$

To multiply most two-figure numbers by 11, separate the two figures, add them together and put the answer between the two figures.

Example:

$26 \times 11 = 28\underset{(2 + 6)}{\underbrace{\phantom{xx}}}6$

$43 \times 11 = 47\underset{(4 + 3)}{\underbrace{\phantom{xx}}}3$

(This works for all numbers whose two figures add up to less than 10.)

## ME OR I?

If you never know whether to say 'I' or 'me', this hint might help. If the word comes after 'and' – as in 'Jim and I' or 'Jim and me', see what happens if you drop the other person. 'Jim and I went for a walk' is right, because 'I went for a walk' sounds good. 'Jim and me went for a walk' is wrong, because 'me went for a walk' is obviously incorrect. In this case 'I' is the *subject* – the person *doing* something.

'Mum gave some cake to Jim and me' is right. ('Mum gave some cake to me.') 'Mum gave some cake to Jim and I' is wrong. ('Mum gave some cake to I.') In this case, '*me*' is the *object* – the person to whom something is *done*.

## MEASURING

Use your body as a measuring guide. Use a ruler or tape to measure:

(a) the distance between your little finger and thumb (with your hand spread out),

(b) the length of your shoe, and

(c) your normal stride, from the heel of your back foot to the heel of your front.

Remember these measurements and you'll always be able to make a rough guess when there's no tape measure around. (Re-measure every now and then, as you grow bigger.)

## MEDICINE
If you have to take medicine which tastes nasty, suck an ice-cube first, to numb your tongue.

## MEMORY
If you want to remember to take something with you when you go out, stick a note to the back of the door you'll be going out by.

## MESSAGES
A length of garden hose makes quite a good speaking tube. Talk down one end and see if you can be heard at the other. If so, use it from room to room, or between different parts of the garden. Blowing a whistle down one end should attract attention when you want to talk to someone.

## MICE
Don't give cheese to pet mice. It makes them smell (worse).

## MODELLING
Make your own modelling dough by mixing three cups of flour, one cup of salt, one cup of water and a little food colouring. Knead the mixture thoroughly. The dough will keep soft for several days if you keep it in a plastic bag in the fridge.

*Use it from room to room . . .*

## MUSIC

Guitar strings are tuned to the notes E, A, D, G, B and E. To remember this, say:

*Eat At Dan's — Good Bacon and Eggs.*

Violin strings are tuned to GDAE:

*Good Dogs Aid Elephants.*

The notes on lines of music can be remembered like this:

Treble lines: *Every Good Boy Deserves Fireworks*
Treble spaces: *FACE*
Bass lines: *Good Boys Deserve Fruit Always*
Bass spaces: *All Cows Eat Grass*

## MUSIC TAPES

A broken music tape can be stuck together with a spot of nail polish remover. Overlap the broken ends, making sure you keep the tape straight, dab on the nail polish remover and pinch to join firmly until it holds.

## NIGHTSHIRTS

Girls – ask your father or older brother for any cast-off shirts. They make great nightshirts.

## NUMBERS

To remember a number (such as a telephone number), think of a rhyme for each figure. For instance 381 could be 'She hates fun', or 409 6582 could be 'You're so fine, vicar, I've dated you'.

The rhyme doesn't have to be very good – 'vicar', for instance, couldn't be anything but six.

## ON BOARD

Port and starboard – which is left and which is right? PORT is LEFT – they have the same number of letters.

## ORANGES

Always peel oranges from the stalk end, and the pith will come away with the peel.

## PAINTING

When colouring or painting, work downwards from the top to avoid smudging. It also helps if you keep a clean piece of paper under your hand.

Keep one paintbrush just for white.

Plastic egg-boxes can be used as paint-mixing trays.

To keep your favourite drawing or painting from fading or smudging, give it a good coating of hairspray.

## PILLS
A pinch of salt on the back of your tongue can help when you have difficulty swallowing a pill.

Or cover the pill in butter.

If you have to give your dog or cat a pill, try disguising the pill in a blob of cream cheese or liver sausage.

## PING-PONG BALLS
A dented ping-pong ball can be restored to its proper shape by putting it in hot, salted water.

*Put it in hot, salted water . . .*

## PLANETS
To remember the order of the planets, going outwards from the sun, say: Mary Very Early Made Jane Shake Up Nellie's Pillow. (*Mercury, Venus, Earth, Mars, Jupiter, Saturn, Uranus, Neptune, Pluto.*)

## PLASTIC BAGS
To open a plastic bag that seems to be stuck, roll the cut edges briskly between your palms.

## POTATO
Cold boiled potato makes a good emergency substitute for sticky paste because the starch in it acts as a glue.

## PRESENTS
Quick and easy presents that are always welcome are drink mats made from pretty tiles. Tile shops will often let you have one or two tiles from left-over stock very cheaply. All you have to do then is stick a corn pad or a small piece of felt to each corner of the base and you have a drink mat that won't damage tables.

If you need to wrap a present and haven't any proper wrapping paper, use kitchen foil.

## PROJECTS
Take care to present a project as neatly as possible, in your best writing and with clearly labelled pictures. Even if the content isn't all that good, you'll get marks for its appearance.

## PURSES
To carry a purse safely when you're wearing trousers, fix the zip of the purse to a belt loop with a key ring, so that the purse can hang down inside your pocket.

If you have no pocket, a purse with a shoulder strap can be worn under your clothes.

## PYJAMAS
If your pyjama trousers are worn out or too short, cut the legs off at the knee and have shortie pyjamas for summer.

## RABBITS
Never pick up a rabbit by its ears. Always place one hand beneath its hindquarters, and steady its head and ears with the other.

*Never pick up a rabbit by its ears . . .*

Crisp, dry autumn leaves can be used as bedding for rabbits.

Stale bread dried in the oven makes excellent crusts for pet rabbits and rodents. Your pets will keep their teeth healthy and blunt and enjoy a good gnaw at the same time.

## RAINBOWS
The colours of the rainbow are Red, Orange, Yellow, Green, Blue, Indigo, Violet.

Remember them by saying, 'Rip Off Your Garters Before I Vomit' or 'Richard of York Gained Battle in Vain'.

## RECORDS
If a record album is slightly warped, you should be able to flatten it by placing it between two sheets of glass and leaving it in the sun for a day on a flat surface.

To help you identify record singles easily, stick a picture of the pop star concerned on to the record sleeve.

## RHINOS
*What to do if you're charged by a rhinoceros:* Keep still until the very last moment, then dodge to one side. A rhino has a very narrow field of vision and won't know where you've gone. It's also not capable of making sharp turns when it's at full gallop.

*Dodge to one side . . .*

## RIGHT AND LEFT

Can you tell your right hand from your left hand? If you're right-handed, say, 'My RIGHT hand is the hand I WRITE with.' If you're left-handed, say, 'I WRITE with the hand that's LEFT.'

## ROYALTY

What to do if you meét the Queen: bow . . . or curtsey.

Shake hands only if she offers her hand to you first. Call her 'Your Majesty' to start with, then 'Ma'am' (that's 'Mam as in jam, not Marm as in palm').

If you are a boy and you meet a member of the royal family, you should bow with your head only. Don't bend at the waist. Girls should give a little curtsey.

*Don't bend at the waist . . .*

To write a formal letter to the Prince of Wales, it is correct to begin like this:

Sir,

and to end like this:

I have the honour to be,
Sir,
Your Royal Highness's most
humble and obedient servant,

## RUBBER BANDS
Old rubber gloves can be cut up to make rubber bands. Make tiny ones from the fingers and big ones from the wrists.

## SANDWICHES
*What to do with stale sandwiches:* Beat together 1 egg and 3 tablespoons of milk, dip the sandwiches into this mixture then fry them in oil or butter until they are golden on both sides. Delicious.

## SCHOOL
If you need to ask your parents for permission to take something to school the next day, always ask the night before. You're more likely then to get yes for an answer than if you leave it until the morning.

To avoid chaos on school mornings, pack your school bag the night before.

*Ask someone to distract you . . .*

## SEASICKNESS

If you suffer from this, remember to take a travel sickness pill beforehand. Stay in the fresh air, if you can, and ask someone to do their best to distract you. The worst thing for you is to keep moaning and groaning about it.

## SEWING

If you're sewing, and the needle tends to stick, run it carefully through your hair for a few seconds, to 'oil' it.

To prevent thread from tangling when you're sewing, always thread it so that the end you've cut from the reel is furthest from the needle.

## SHAMPOO

Shampoo mixed with soda water will go further, as the fizz produces lots of lather.

If you hate getting shampoo in your eyes, smear Vaseline above your eyebrows. The Vaseline will act as a water barrier.

## SHOES

Brown shoes can be given a quick clean with the inside of a banana skin. Leave them to dry then polish with a soft cloth.

Rub scuffed shoes with a piece of raw potato before putting on the polish. They'll shine like new.

Spray-on furniture polish makes a speedy shoe-shine.

*Emergency treatment for scuffed shoes:* Cover the scuffs and scratches with matching felt-tip pen, then coat with furniture polish or shoe wax.

Tennis shoes can be cleaned with a soap-filled scouring pad (such as a Brillo pad). You can help them stay clean by spraying them with starch.

If your shoelaces lose their plastic tabs and become frayed and hard to thread, tidy the ends with sticky tape. You could also try painting them with clear glue. When they're almost dry, press them firmly into points.

## SLEEP

If you find it hard to get to sleep, concentrate on relaxing one bit of you at a time: first one foot, then the other, then your ankles, then your knees, and so on, until every limb is floppy. When you get to your head, unclench your teeth and feel your forehead smoothing out.

Now imagine yourself lying on a beach with a warm breeze blowing over you, and you'll soon be asleep.

*Back steadily away . . .*

## SNAKES

If you're sleeping outside in an area where there are likely to be snakes, arrange a rough, hairy rope in a circle right round your sleeping area. Snakes hate crossing anything prickly.

If you come face to face with a wild cobra, it's no good shouting at it – cobras are deaf! Make no sudden movements, but back steadily away, then run.

Don't be afraid of performing snakes – almost all have had their teeth taken out or their venom removed.

## SNEEZING
If you feel a sneeze coming on, and you want to stop it, touch the roof of your mouth firmly with the tip of your tongue.

Alternatively, press a finger firmly on the end of your nose and push upwards.

## SNOW
Make snow pictures by pressing your water colour paintings face down in flat snow. The designs will be printed on to the snow.

## SPAGHETTI
Does spaghetti get the better of you? Try using a fork in your right hand and a soup spoon in your left (or the other way around, if you're left-handed).

*Twizzle it round and round . . .*

Pick up the spaghetti with the fork, and use the spoon to stop the spaghetti falling off the fork while you twizzle it round and round. Just before you put it in your mouth, tip the fork up and away from the spoon.

## SPECTACLES
To clean spectacles, rub a drop of vinegar over both sides of the lenses, then polish with a soft cloth.

## SPELLING
You know there's an **I** and an **E**, but is it **IE** or **EI**? The rule is:

*'I before E except after C, where the vowels make the sound "EE".'*

This will help you to spell words like bel**IE**f, n**IE**ce and rec**EI**ve.

Is it stationery or stationary? Station**AR**y means standing still like a p**AR**ked c**AR**. Station**ER**y is what a station**ER** sells, which means things like pap**ER**.

Some words are easier to spell than they sound, so long as you remember that the difficult bits are all double letters. For example:

MISSISSIPPI
COMMITTEE
ACCOMMODATE

## SPIDERS
If you're lost, and don't know in which direction you're heading, look out for spiders' webs on bushes. Spiders usually make webs on the south side, which is warmer.

*Spiders are good weather forecasters . . .*

Spiders are good weather forecasters. When it's about to rain they shorten the threads that support their webs.

To stop spiders climbing up the plug-hole, smear it with soap (or leave the plug in).

## SPLINTERS
Before removing a splinter from your finger, try soaking it in baby oil. That way the splinter should come out more easily.

## STAGE FRIGHT

As you stand trembling in the wings, waiting to go on stage, cup your hands in front of your nose and mouth and blow out all your breath. Now breathe it all back in again.

Do this a few times and you should feel able to tackle anything. Apparently the carbon dioxide in your 'used' breath nudges the adrenal glands into action. These produce adrenalin, which helps you to handle stress. (It might work for exam nerves, too.)

## STAMPS

If you hate the taste of glue on the backs of stamps, lick the envelope instead.

*For stamp-collectors:* To peel a stamp off an envelope, rub the inside of the envelope (behind the stamp) with surgical spirit on a piece of cotton wool.

Stamps or labels that are stuck together are easier to separate if you put them in the freezer for half an hour.

## STICKING PLASTER

To remove it painlessly, dissolve the glue little by little by rubbing with cotton wool soaked in surgical spirit.

## STICKY MARKS

Use nail polish remover to get rid of the stickiness left from posters and labels stuck on to windows.

## STICKY TAPE

When you finish using sticky tape, slip a button under the cut end of the roll and it'll be easy to find the end next time.

## STINGS

To relieve nettle stings, rub the painful area with rosemary, mint, sage or dock leaves.

## STITCHES
If you get a 'stitch in your side', bend down and touch your toes a few times, then try to breathe very regularly.

## STRING
When tying a parcel with string, wet the string first and it will dry taut.

## SUNBURN
If you've been out in the sun too long, you can cool down sunburnt areas with a wet tea bag.

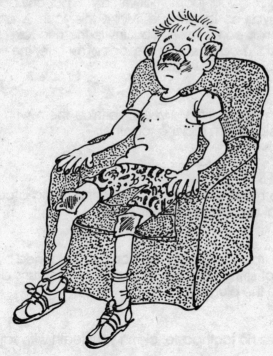

*Cool down sunburnt areas . . .*

## SURNAMES
Some names are not pronounced the way they're written.
Examples are:

Beauchamp (pronounced Beecham)
Beaulieu (pronounced Bewly)
Cadogan (pronounced Kerduggan)
Cholmondeley (pronounced Chumly)
Colquhoun (pronounced Cahoon)
Mainwaring (pronounced Mannering)
Sandys (pronounced Sands)

## SWAPPING
Keep a box in your room into which you put any books or
toys that you no longer use. Make this your 'Swap Box'.
When friends come to see you, invite them to take something from the box they like the look of, or offer the various
bits and pieces as swaps.

## SWEETS
If you're making sticky sweets, sprinkle them with icing-
sugar to stop them sticking together.

## TADPOLES
They love meat, so tie a piece of string round a cube of
lean meat and hang it in their tank.

## TAPS
The noise from a dripping tap can be deadened by tying
a piece of string from the tap so that water runs down it
straight to the plughole.

## TEETH
If you have no toothpaste, clean your teeth with salt.

Cleaning your teeth with bicarbonate of soda makes them whiter.

If you have a loose tooth, don't wiggle it at people – eat a toffee to get rid of it.

*Don't wiggle it at people . . .*

## TEXTBOOKS
An old road map makes a great cover for a school textbook.

## TIES

If you have trouble tying a tie, wrap it around your thigh and tie it facing you. When you've got it right, slip it off your leg, drop it over your head and tighten it.

When you remove your school tie, just loosen it enough so that it slips over your head. That way you won't have to knot it again the next day.

## TIRED LEGS

If your legs are tired, stand first on one leg, then the other, holding the 'spare' leg up with your hand, to give it a rest.

## TOMATOES

Tomatoes stay firmer if you slice them from top to bottom, not across their middles.

## TOOLBOXES

Mothballs, charcoal or chalk kept in a toolbox help prevent rust.

## TOOTHPASTE

Use it to stick posters to walls without causing any damage to the paint or wallpaper. (It should wash off quite easily, but do ask permission first.)

To squeeze out the last little bit of toothpaste, warm the tube in hot water then wrap it tightly around a pencil.

## TORCHES

If you need to use a torch in the rain, put it in a clear plastic bag, sealed with a rubber band. You can still turn it on and off, and the light will shine clearly through the plastic.

## TRAVELLING

To save space when travelling by car, pack your clothes

*Make your suitcase easy to identify . . .*

and soft toys into pillowcases and use them as pillows on the journey.

When travelling by air, it's a good idea to make your suitcase easy to identify by sticking coloured tape along the top or tying a bright ribbon to the handle.

## WALKING

If you're out in the dark, wear something light so that you can be seen on the road.

You can walk further and be less tired if you turn up your toes. This helps you to begin your step firmly on your heel before transferring the weight to the ball of your foot.

Going on a sponsored walk? To prevent blisters, protect the pressure points (heels, balls of feet, little toes) with sticking plasters. You can also try rubbing the insides of the heels of your socks with soap.

*Paint it once a day . . .*

## WARTS
To get rid of a wart, paint it once a day with nail varnish until it dries up and goes away.

## WATERMELONS
To test a watermelon for ripeness, try the 'Pink-punk' test. Snap your fingers against the melon. If it says a shrill 'Pink!' it isn't ripe. If it says a low 'Punk!' it's ready to eat.

## WATER PISTOLS
Empty washing-up bottles make good water pistols.

## WELLIES
To dry wet wellies, use a hairdryer.

Wellies can be cold in winter. Protect your feet from the cold by cutting several thicknesses of newspaper to the shape of your feet and placing them inside the boots.

Another way to keep your feet warm inside your wellies is to wear plastic bags over your socks.

## WOODLICE
*How to catch a woodlouse:* Cut a potato in half and hollow it out. Put it face down on the ground and wood-lice will soon collect in it. Take them to the compost heap, where they'll do a great job in breaking down the vegetation.

## WOODWORK
The golden rule for woodworkers is 'Measure twice and cut once.' In other words, make quite sure you've measured correctly before you begin to cut the wood.

When cutting plywood, prevent it from splitting by sticking masking tape along the line you plan to saw. Saw through the plywood and the tape at the same time.

When nailing two pieces of wood together, always nail through the thinner piece into the thicker piece.

To keep a nail steady as you hammer it, push it through a

*Hold the edge of the card . . .*

piece of card and hold the edge of the card. Tear the card away when the nail is firm.

Rub a screw or a nail against a bar of soap and it will go more easily into wood.

*To clean wood-shavings from a file:* Press a piece of masking tape over the blade. As you pull it away, the shavings will come off with it.

If you are constructing something using small parts, such as screws, stick them on to a length of sticky tape so they don't get lost, or keep them in an ice-cube tray.

## WRITING

When writing on unlined paper, place a sheet of lined paper underneath, to help you keep your writing straight. If you can't see the lines well enough, go over them with a thick black pen and ruler. Keep your line guide to use the next time.

## ZIPS

Does your zip stick? Try rubbing it with a lead pencil or a piece of candle wax.

# Part Two:
# FAMILY, FRIENDS AND YOU

## ASKING FAVOURS

*How to ask for something you want:*

Rule number one – pick a good moment.

Rule number two – smile.

Rule number three – say 'please'.

If you begin by saying, 'Could you do me a favour?' or 'Can I ask a favour?' you're more likely to get a good

*Say 'please' . . .*

response than if you dive straight in with, 'Can I stay up late tonight?' Asking someone for a favour makes them feel more generous and kindly.

## KEEPING YOUR COOL
If you have a quick temper, you'll have heard the advice about counting to ten before reacting to something that upsets you. Breathe deeply while counting and some of the anger will go away.

## SAYING SORRY
If you can't bring yourself to go up to someone and say it, just write 'Sorry' on a bit of paper and hand it to them or leave it on their desk. If you can't say sorry and mean it, or at least want to make friends again, don't say it.

One way to say sorry is to show how you feel by doing something thoughtful for the other person.

## DEALING WITH BULLIES
Bullies are usually people who feel inferior to others in some way and try to hide this by bullying. They hope this makes them appear strong.

Try not to appear scared of bullies, as this encourages them. Keep out of their way, if you can, but if you're not able to do this, stick up for yourself. Bullies are usually cowards. Get a teacher or some of your friends on your side and the bully will probably leave you alone.

If the bully goes on annoying you, walk away and join your friends or an adult.

Above all, don't be afraid to tell a grown-up. If the bully then gets into trouble, he or she may sneer at you afterwards, but will think twice before bullying you again. *This does not count as sneaking.* You are simply protecting yourself and other people, rather than protecting the bully.

*Stick up for yourself . . .*

## LEAVING FOOD

If you're not at home and you're offered something to eat that you simply can't stand, *never* say straight out, 'I don't like it.' You are likely to offend the cook, even if it's not his or her fault. Just say politely, 'None for me, thank you.'

If the food is already on your plate, try a little if you can, otherwise just leave it. There's no need to mention it at all, but if you *are* asked, 'Don't you like it?' you can always say 'Sorry, I know it's stupid, but I'm not all that keen on it.'

Some people are more adventurous about food than others, and it certainly helps to avoid awkward moments if you do your best to eat most things.

Never give up on a food you think you don't like. Our tastes change as we grow older, and if you hated, say, mushrooms when you were little, you may love them now. But you'll never find out unless you do a taste check from time to time.

*Try a little if you can . . .*

## BAD MOODS

If someone is in a bad mood, avoid them. The bad mood probably has nothing to do with you, and is more likely to go away of its own accord if left alone.

If you have bad moods yourself, try not to inflict them on other people. Keep away from them until you feel more sociable.

*If someone is in a bad mood . . .*

## FEELING SICK
If you feel sick, or feel a cough coming on when you need
to be quiet, or you want to prevent yourself crying, breathe
deeply in and out through your mouth.

## IN THE DOGHOUSE
If your parents are cross with you, decide on some little
thing you can do that will put you back in their good books.
Sometimes all it needs is a corner of your room tidied, or
a cup washed up – and suddenly you're in favour
again.

## MAKING FRIENDS

To be accepted into a circle of friends in a new school, try to find out their interests and swot up on one of them. Then you'll have something to talk about – but make sure you don't sound too much of a know-all!

## HOMESICKNESS

At the end of every day, don't think: 'I'm one day further from home', think: 'I'm one day nearer'. In other words, from the moment you leave home, count the days till you return, rather than the time you've been away.

## AFTER THE STORM

If you've stormed off to your room in a temper, it can be embarrassing to come down and face the family again. Remember that they'll be pleased to see you – no one can relax when one person is in a mood. Just come down as though nothing's happened and head for the person who's most likely to give you a quick hug and make you feel less silly. They'll all know how you feel – it happens to everyone from time to time.

## TEASING

Children only tease to get you annoyed – not to hurt you (though teasing does sometimes hurt). The best way to deal with teasing is to ignore it. The teasers will soon get bored and go elsewhere.

If you want to annoy a teaser back, simply smile at him. Nothing is more infuriating!

## SAYING NO

Suppose your friends ask you to do something you don't want to do. You refuse. They call you a sissy:

*You:* 'Think what you like. I don't care.'
*Friend:* 'I won't be your friend, then.'

*Simply smile at him . . .*

*You* (walking away): 'So who needs friends like you? I've got others.'

If all else fails, you can always say, 'Anyway, I know something you don't know.' Even if the other person pretends not to care, it will irritate him or her that you might, in fact, know some interesting secret.

If a grown-up asks you do something you feel is wrong, it can be hard to refuse without seeming rude. But you *can* refuse, and you should, as firmly and politely as possible. As soon as you can, tell a sympathetic adult (your teacher, perhaps). Don't be afraid that no one will be on your side – they will probably be more understanding than you think.

If a total stranger tries to persuade you to do anything at all, just shout 'No!' in your loudest voice and run away.

## HOW TO BE POPULAR

Try to be nice to everyone – not only your close friends.

Smile a lot.

Be interested in other people.

Make people feel good about themselves.

Don't say nasty things behind anyone's back – others will think you might do it to *them*.

Be a generous winner and a good loser.


## REMEMBERING THINGS

How's your memory? In the old days almost everyone carried a handkerchief. If you wanted to remember something you could tie a knot in your handkerchief, which would at least remind you that you needed to remember *something*. If you tend to be forgetful, or if you remember things – but at the wrong time – here's a really good memory trick:

Make a picture in your head of whatever it is you want to remember, together with a picture of something you know you'll be seeing at the time you need to do the remembering.

For instance, let's say you want to remember to feed the neighbours' goldfish. You remember this while you're out shopping, but that's no use at all – you need to remember it when you get home. What do you usually do when you get home? Hang your coat on a hook?

Picture the empty hook. Now picture a label hanging from it, saying 'Goldfish'.

Perhaps you want to remember to feed them before you begin watching the television. Think of goldfish swimming across the TV screen.

When you get home, as soon as you go to hang up your

coat or turn on the TV, you'll think, 'Oh yes, I must feed next door's goldfish.'

## SHOUTING
If someone is shouting at you, don't shout back. Whisper at them. They'll probably keep quiet to try to hear what you're saying.

## GETTING EVEN
*What to do if someone is beastly to you:* Imagine that above everyone's head is a big bucket of revolting gunge. Every time that person is unkind, the bucket fills up a bit more. When the bucket is full, it tips its load on to the person's head. Of course, gunge won't really plop down

*Knickers falling down in rounders . . .*

from the sky, but you can await with glee the downfall that is sure to come in due course to your tormentor. What would you plan for them if you could?

*An own goal at football?*

*A slip in a big cowpat?*

*Knickers falling down in rounders?*

*Being told off in front of everyone at assembly?*

*Falling flat in gym?*

*Having a worst secret told round the school?*

Imagining that a ghastly fate is on its way will help you not to mind so much.

## CHOOSING

If you're offered a choice – for instance, 'Would you like crisps or peanuts?' – try to make up your mind quickly. Don't feel that one choice will be more trouble than another. Most of all, don't say, 'I don't mind' (even if it's true). Though this is meant to be a helpful statement, it's just irritating.

## MEETING PEOPLE

If you're nervous about entering a room full of people, don't think, 'What will *they* think of *me*?', think 'What will *I* think of *them*?'

In other words, they're just like you – far more worried about how they themselves appear to everyone else. Remember that most people want to like and be liked.

## HOW TO ANSWER BACK

Do people sometimes call you names?

First of all – what *not* to do. Don't go red in the face, burst into tears and run away. That's just what the name-caller wants. The trouble is, sometimes you *have* to run away, because you can't think what else to do. If this happens to you quite often, a good answer is to practise a few put-downs, so that when someone calls you Thickhead or Fatso or anything else that hurts, you can come straight back at them with:

'Takes one to know one.'

'Go play on the motorway!'

'Have you looked in the mirror lately?'

'Take a long walk off a short pier.'

'Oh look, something's escaped from the zoo!'

'I'd rather have snot for a friend than you.'

*Practise a few put-downs . . .*

A comment on the colour of your skin deserves total contempt:

*'So what else is new?'*

*'Brilliantly original!'*

If someone threatens you, try:

*'You and whose army?'*

If someone says you smell, say:

*'So do roses!'*

Whatever the name you're called, *stand your ground*, and if you can't think of anything else, just say,

*'Push off, birdbrain!'*

It'll make you feel a lot better, and, with a bit of luck, they'll go and find someone else to be mean to.

## SAYING THANK YOU

If someone sends you a present, or you've been to a party, do remember to say thank you. It's best to write a short note – just a few lines will do – or you should at least ring up the next day.

If you don't say thank you:

a) The sender of the present won't know if it arrived safely.

b) The giver might think you didn't like the present or enjoy the party.

c) You may be considered rude and thoughtless.

d) You'll be lucky to receive a present or invitation again.

Most people don't give presents just to get thanked, and often they're nice enough not to mind if you forget to thank them, but have you ever given something to someone, or done something for somebody, and not been thanked?

Were your feelings hurt? Did you feel taken for granted? Grown-ups have feelings, too, and like to feel appreciated from time to time.

## HOW TO BE A FAILURE
If you're not very good at something, even though you've really tried, it's best to admit it. Make a joke of it if that helps. You can't be good at everything – *nobody* is – and you may well find you can be good at something that most other people can't manage.

Sometimes we don't find out what we're best at until long after we've left school. Early no-hopers at schoolwork who became hugely successful include Sir Winston Churchill, Richard Branson and Princess Diana, so just be patient and wait for your talents to emerge. Your turn will come.

## AND FINALLY . . .
Some very old hints that are *not* recommended:

'If you get the cramp, wear on your naked leg the skin of an eel.'

'Sufferers from dandruff and greasy hair should not wash the hair more than once every three weeks.'

'To cure the colic (tummy ache), stand on your head for a quarter of an hour.'

'If you suffer with a stye in your eye, pull one hair from the tail of a black cat on the first night of the new moon, then rub the tip of the tail nine times over the affected part.'

*Pull one hair from the tail . . .*

'An asthma attack will quickly respond to a spoonful of castor oil.'

'For the ague (shivering fits), wrap a spider in a raisin and swallow it whole.'

'Thrash your chilblains with holly, keeping your legs crossed while doing so, and the chilblains will disappear.'

'Swallowing baby frogs before breakfast will bring relief to those with consumption (a disease of the lungs).'

'By far the best thing for whooping cough is a meal of crushed snails and minced mice.'

'Playing tennis is an excellent cure for blushing.'

## THE FAMOUS FIVE DIARY

### AN ACTION PACKED DIARY WITH SPACE FOR ALL YOUR FACTS AND SECRETS!

Plot the year ahead with The Famous Five! There's space for your facts and secrets, games to play, nature information, special days and festivals to celebrate and lots more!

Make this year the best ever with the help of Anne, Dick, George (Georgina), Julian – and Timmy too!

**KNIGHT BOOKS**

# SURVIVAL! A SCHOOL KID'S GUIDE

## GLADYS OVER

### DANGER SIGNS!

Do you feel unwell most Monday mornings, but on top of the world on Friday afternoons? Do your eyes water when it's liver and bacon for lunch but light up when it's sausage and beans?

Are you revolted when your teacher asks you the difference between a toad and an earthworm, but revived when they suggest you might do a nature study in the park for a change?

Then look out! These are the symptoms of a severely distressed pupil. If you are to survive school, you must take action right now.

### APPROVED CURE:

Read this in depth guide on how to last out until the bell rings. Whether you suffer from brainboxes, cheating, dinner ladies, ink pellets, jelly or yawning, you need worry no longer. Here is your essential SURVIVAL GUIDE.

**KNIGHT BOOKS**

# THE RAINY DAY SURVIVAL BOOK

## JEREMY TAPSCOTT

This book is here to save you. Packed with 1001 cheap, easy and fun things to do – not just on rainy days but during thunderstorms and even a monsoon! Simply showered with illustrations and positively downpoured with original ideas.

**KNIGHT BOOKS**

# THE RIGHT IMPRESSION

## GARY WILMOT

The Duchess of York, Jimmy Cricket, Mrs Thatcher *and* Madonna in your living room? They could be if you follow Gary Wilmot's advice and make – THE RIGHT IMPRESSION!

**KNIGHT BOOKS**